How to Analyze People through Body Language

Learn how to use Microexpressions and body language to analyze people and identify personality types

By Edward Brandon

express consent of the Publisher is provided beforehand. Any additional rights reserved.

Furthermore, the information that can be found within the pages described forthwith shall be considered both accurate and truthful when it comes to the recounting of facts. As such, any use, correct or incorrect, of the provided information will render the Publisher free of responsibility as to the actions taken outside of their direct purview. Regardless, there are zero scenarios where the original author or the Publisher can be deemed liable in any fashion for any damages or hardships that may result from any of the information discussed herein.

Additionally, the information in the following pages is intended only for informational purposes and should thus be thought of as universal. As befitting its nature, it is presented without assurance regarding its prolonged validity or interim quality. Trademarks that are mentioned are done without written consent and can in no way be considered an endorsement from the trademark holder.

Table of Contents

INTRODUCTION 11

CHAPTER 1: EMOTIONAL MANIPULATION, GASLIGHTING, AND HOW TO PROTECT YOURSELF 15

Gaslighting 20
How to Protect Yourself 22

CHAPTER 2: ANALYZING PEOPLE 32

CHAPTER 3: MICROEXPRESSIONS AND BODY LANGUAGE 49

CHAPTER 4: PERSONALITY TYPES 62

Sensing (S) – Intuition (I) 64
Thinking (T) – Feeling (F) 65
Judging (J) – Perceiving (P) 66
The 16 Personality Types 67
   The Inspector 67
   The Counselor 68
   The Mastermind 69
   The Giver 70
   The Craftsman 71
   The Provider 72
   The Idealist 73
   The Performer 74
   The Champion 75
   The Doer 75
   The Supervisor 76
   The Commander 77
   The Thinker 77
   The Nurturer 78
   The Visionary 79
   The Composer 79

CHAPTER 5: INFLUENCE HUMAN BEHAVIOR 82

Human Behavior 83
Influence, Persuasion, Manipulation, and Coercion 84
   Influence 84
   Persuasion 84
   Manipulation 87

Coercion *91*

CONCLUSION..**97**

Introduction

The following chapters will discuss the core concepts behind manipulation and dark psychology—what it is, the different strategies and philosophies behind its practice, real-world examples to thoroughly illustrate each topic, and research examples that back up the application of these practices.

As you read this book, you will discover the hidden worlds of the human psyche and the power innate in all of us, waiting to be tapped and analyzed.

In chapter 1, we will switch gears a bit to focus solely on how you can personally protect yourself against dark psychology and manipulation techniques. Everything that you learn in this area will work to your benefit as you train your brain to pick up on the subtle signals that someone is trying to manipulate you in some way.

You will recognize them because you've read about them, and you've analyzed many examples of these practices in action.

Some people are simply not very practiced, but others, like some of the famous psychopathic killers that people discuss for decades after they've been convicted of their crimes, probably spent their entire lives honing these skills automatically as a means to satisfy their natures and the desires and fears inherent in their personality disorders.

It is a fascinating topic, but it is also one that deserves a great deal of respect—lest you find yourself trusting the wrong person or getting sucked in by someone's "charm."

Chapter 2 gets into the technicalities involved with analyzing people, down to the details. You will be introduced to such topics as cold reading, mirroring, and understanding the human character in its various shapes and forms.

We will discuss how society has shaped human nature and instinct—sometimes for the better, and oftentimes for the worst.

Microexpressions and body language are the topics of chapter 3, in which we will look closely at some examples of people meeting in the real world to analyze how they interact and how you can learn to pick up on things that people usually never even notice, except for in their subconscious minds.

Learn what to look for in order to get a feel for the kind of impression you are making on another person. We will look specifically at these signals taking place in a situation where a man is trying to engage and flirt with a woman in the dating scene.

In chapter 4, we will give you a thorough analysis of the personality types as outlined and established by Katharine Cook Briggs and her daughter Isabel Briggs Myers.

These indicators are put together in groups of 4 to determine your personality type based on your answers to a series of questions.

We will take a look at how to read and understand each of these indicators, as well as a brief discussion of several of the personality types and their frequency of occurrence in the American population today.

Chapter 1: Emotional Manipulation, Gaslighting, and How to Protect Yourself

Human emotions can take hold of a person and influence his/her actions, even superseding all sense of logic and reason. We are driven to act through emotions like anger, love, and jealousy.

Sometimes, the steps we take are impossible to take back, and an endless list of stories serve as cautionary tales against letting your emotions run away with you before thinking things through.

When it comes to influence and control, emotional manipulation is one of the most potent tools a practitioner of dark psychology can use, as someone who succumbs to emotion will abandon logic and reason for the sake of satiating whatever feelings are eating away at them.

For example, a person who is so attached to another that she will abandon all other relationships for the sake of holding onto a partner is a prime example of someone who has fallen under the spell of emotional manipulation.

No genuinely caring and loving partner would ask a spouse or girlfriend to abandon the positive relationship with her family, but her actions of doing so at her partner's request show that her attachment and dependence on such a partner has gone beyond rational thought that might lead her to make a better decision in her own interest.

Creating emotional dependence requires consistency and patience. Once the practitioner has his target, he will begin the process with personifying this idea of a perfect partner as we discussed in the last chapter.

The object is to portray a seemingly ideal partner who is caring, loving, selfless, and showers her with compliments and gifts, including his own time. Whatever it is she desires, he gives it to her to the best of his ability.

This creates an almost intoxicating bond with the partner, and she will end up doing everything she can to make him happy in return.

The effect of this type of bond and addiction is that when the manipulator starts pulling away, the target will feel desperate anxiety about losing the attention she's grown accustomed to. This is the next step in the game as the manipulator plays on her attachment. He will make an excuse about needing to pull away or put some space between them, but he is careful to maintain some communication, perhaps in the form of text messages or emails, so that there is still an attachment and she doesn't decide to cut things off altogether.

The amount of time he pulls away depends on the situation, but eventually, he will come back to her arms, which gives her a massive dose of what she has been craving, all of those feelings come flooding back to her.

Next, the manipulator will create a stronger bond between them in some way. He will probably return to the level of attention he had offered in the past, but it is essential to keep working toward a stronger relationship, just as natural relationships continue to get stronger with continued time and patience and working through hardships.

He will open up to her and explain whatever feelings or tumult he is going through that is causing him to push away. This creates sympathy in his partner that she will hold on to the next time he pulls away, which will be soon.

This routine is repeated, but not always overtly. It is possible to pull away emotionally and not physically, which also works to create a feeling of missing the emotional bond the partners usually shared.

This practice will work differently and to varying degrees based on the person involved, but the results can be quite insidious. An added dimension of the emotional dependency manipulation is that once that insatiable addiction is created, the manipulator can then start to ask things of his partner in return for his affection, though it is not an overt transaction.

These things are expressed through heartfelt conversation, and the target is led gently towards the conclusion that she must do this for her partner, or give up that to win him back, etc.

Perhaps he creates a competitive situation in which he expresses that he is fighting his attraction for another woman and if she just did this or that thing or dedicated her time to whatever task he chooses, then she could win him for good.

This is only one example of many possibilities that open up once the manipulator has his target under his spell.

Gaslighting

As we move away from emotional manipulation a bit, there is another tactic associated with dark psychology, which can have debilitating results on the target.

Though establishing emotional dependency before engaging a gaslighting tactic can make the effects much stronger, it is not necessary for the independent mental harm that results from a successful gaslighting attempt.

Successful gaslighting can happen intentionally or unintentionally. Let's first get a clearer idea of precisely what gaslighting is before we look at some examples of how this happens.

Gaslighting is an effect over time that happens when someone causes the victim to question his/her life through consistent denial of the reality he/she experiences. A victim may initially fight back harshly, but, over time, as the behavior remains the same parallel to the abuse, the victim may become confused and belittled as they start to question themselves, even though they had been so sure of what they'd experienced.

For example, a mother says harsh things passive-aggressively to her daughter, but the next day when the daughter works up the courage to address her behavior, the mother denies that she did any such thing.

The daughter might cry and yell and curse and try everything she can to get her mother to acknowledge the pain she's inflicted on her, but it never works.

The abuse continues, and the denial continues without the mother budging an inch. Over time, this has a severe emotional and psychological effect that is usually carried as a lifelong burden.

We can never underestimate the power of emotional influence. Once a victim has been broken down emotionally, doors open wide for manipulation techniques.

Similar to the narcissist example where he showers affection then pulls away, the gaslighting victim will develop a kind of desperate need for the manipulator to acknowledge his/her actions, but it never comes.

As mentioned, gaslighting can result unintentionally on the part of the manipulator when he has sufficiently fallen into a routine of denial. When he denies wrongdoing, he allows himself to forget and puts up an impenetrable barrier against the truth.

Even if the victim can show irrefutable proof of what has happened, the manipulator will continue in his denial, causing an incredible amount of frustration and anxiety in the victim.

How to Protect Yourself

When gaslighting occurs during childhood, it is complicated for the defenseless child to protect herself, as the gaslighting would usually be coming from a person of authority or a caregiver, on whom the child depends.

These stories are tragic, and trauma and abuse that is induced during childhood can be particularly long-lasting and severe in its psychological effects.

As we get older, we learn that the world is not full of sincere and well-meaning people, and we learn to be careful about who we trust and give information to.

The extent to which we withhold trust from others varies depending on personality, but most of us have long since learned all about the risks involved with trusting strangers.

Anyone who has had their credit card numbers stolen or has had their car broken into knows that things happen out of opportunity as well as intentional malice.

Those we love have a significant amount of power when it comes to manipulation because the love and trust are there and are waiting to be taken advantage of—if he so chooses.

One of the hardest lessons to wrap your mind around when we talk about protecting oneself from manipulative techniques is to know we don't always completely know people and what's going on in their lives, even if they are family, a partner, or close friend.

There are many stories to cite as examples here, including spouses who end up cheating their spouse's out of money, become verbally and physically abusive, or live a whole separate life outside of his or her partner's awareness.

If you are serious about protecting yourself or believe you may know someone who is practicing gaslighting on a loved one, take some time to think about the warning signs you are getting and how closely they match up with someone who is practicing these manipulation techniques.

One of the first signs of trouble is when a person's moods seem to fluctuate without apparent cause. Perhaps he seems upbeat and happy one minute, then plummets into silence and sullenness the next.

When there is no apparent reason for why this might be happening, you may try to talk to them to figure out what's going on, but they close up and refuse to dialog.

This might be a sign that there is something out of ordinary or wrong with his mental state. It could be a mood disorder, and it could be brewing evil intent.

Whatever the case, and you might not know what's going on yet, it would be good to keep tabs on his behavior and note any additional changes or worsening. This individual could need medical treatment for a mood disorder, among other possibilities.

Another signal to serve as a red flag is when someone does or says something that he is obviously embarrassed about, then immediately seems to forget or deny that he's done any such thing.

This could be an immediate reaction that will develop over time to result in gaslighting where other people are concerned. Denial is a strong defensive response to emotional discomfort and severe stress.

When someone decides they've found a way out of this pain, they may choose to go down the road of denial, as they can consciously force their reality away and create a new one where these things don't exist.

It's like a mental cocoon that people trap themselves in as a way to escape their emotional pain. Many people go through a stage of grief, which is defined by denial of what has happened. Perhaps there was a sudden death, unexpected, and the shock and pain are too much to bear all at once in the moment of discovery.

A common reaction is for the brain to immediately shut down this reality and deny that this event is taking place. It is perfectly normal to go through this stage, as long as the person eventually moves on and continues the grief cycle, which is a healthy response to loss.

Personality changes, denial, and, finally, a pattern of emotional outburst and lack of self-control followed by, if not outright denial yet, playing down his actions to the point that he convinces himself that his behavior wasn't that bad.

For example, a spouse may have gotten drunk and said horrible things to his spouse, but immediately afterward, or later, when his wife brings it up, he will downplay the whole thing having convinced himself he only called her a juvenile name once or twice.

But he didn't say the other things. Those, you're just making up, he would never do that, etc. If he has fallen into a routine of getting drunk and tends to get angry, this could turn into a toxic routine unless the wife figures things out and either gets him immediate help or gets out of the situation.

If any of these behavioral signs crop up in your life, it is advisable that you start really paying attention, and it's probably a good thing to try to talk about what's going on and pinpoint the problem before it gets out of hand. If a person's behavior starts to affect you in a negative way, they have to understand what is happening and that you're not going to tolerate it.

At this point, the individual knows, assuming cognitive capability, that what he is doing is hurting you in some way, and he also knows that if it continues, you are going to leave and not be around to take it anymore.

Depending on the severity of the situation, the person you are trying to get through to may break down and apologize, having just realized the extent to which his behaviors are hurting others—or he may start right in with some of the above-mentioned manipulative techniques in order to get you to stay in his life.

If his hurtful behavior or abuse continues, then you must take action, either to get this person help or to get away from the situation.

If you see a pattern forming and a cycle of abuse getting worse and worse, then you need to get out of the situation.

Call a family member or friend for support. If he continues the violence but then comes back begging for forgiveness and assuring you he will change, then you must recognize the manipulation going on. Is there something you are providing that he doesn't want to love should you leave? Perhaps you are supporting him financially or in some other way. These ties must be severed immediately.

When this happens, the manipulator will often move on to find somebody else who can support him in the same way. He may look for someone else in his purview who might be easy to abuse and manipulate.

Warn your friends and anyone else who might be at risk of his ulterior motives, and then get yourself as far away as possible.

It can be incredibly heartbreaking, but sometimes you have to come to terms at some point with the fact that some people aren't going to change, or "get better," the way you want them to.

Parents with kids who are abusing drugs have a particularly hard time when their children come home, appealing to their parental love as their children, before asking for money that the parents know they will go out and spend on drugs.

What is a parent to do in this situation? There is no easy answer since emotional attachment is one of the most powerful things a human can experience. Sometimes, we make the choice that all the pain is worth having an abuser in our lives.

Others have a breaking point at which they turn away, having had enough of being pulled around and abused.

Catching the warning signs at an early time is the best way to avoid the situation escalating into one where everything is severely getting hurt over and over again as part of a vicious cycle of love, attachment, abuse, and false reconciliation.

Chapter 2: Analyzing People

In this chapter, we will focus on some of the key aspects of the essential step in the practice of dark psychology and manipulation—observation.

Observation in this context does not merely refer to keeping a close eye on potential targets in the vicinity. Paying attention means picking up on details about people that others usually miss when they are not specifically tuned to weed these details out.

If done correctly, the observation step can be accomplished without being noticed, which is essential to not tipping your potential targets off as far as what you're doing or your intentions.

If someone takes a single look at you and think you are creepy, then you can pretty much cross this person off your list of potential targets. People have a subconscious defense when it comes to getting "vibes" from people, so your intention is to remain entirely in the shadows during your observational period of gathering information.

And this is your primary objective. You are watching how your targets interact with each other, what their interests are, their general demeanors.

No detail is too small during this investigative step, but there is also a lot to gain from educating yourself about the basics in terms of human nature and instinct. There are specific universal laws, so to speak, when it comes to social interaction and motivation.

And, though there are exceptions to nearly every rule, having this information will give a considerable advantage when it comes to predicting how a person is going to react when you are finally ready to engage and put a manipulative technique into practice.

One of the fundamentals of the human condition is the desire to connect with other people. Sounds pretty basic, but this means slightly different things to different people. Some people simply desire people to listen to them, while others are singularly focused on finding "the one" with whom they can share the rest of their lives.

Others want to find like-minded people in terms of their areas of interest, which could be anything from scientific theory to their favorite authors.

Some people are naturally open to new friendships and love talking to new people, while others are guarded and tend to shy away from unsolicited attention from strangers.

The one commonality in all of the people, though some show it more than others, is the desire for connection and positive interactions with people.

Loneliness and isolation are key ingredients for the development of depression. Human beings are biologically programmed to be around other people and to have relationships.

Some people may be more challenging to reach, but that doesn't mean that they don't have these same needs and desires.

The observation step is necessary because of the wide variances between people in regard to their openness to new people.

Understanding the social traits of your target will help you when you are ready to make decisions about how you are going to approach your intended target.

If your target is not variable and you need to crack their code individually, then this step is all the more important, especially if they are not very approachable.

Another universal, which we touched on previously, is the fact that, in general, people just want to be entertained. Entertainment means having fun and negating all the negative stuff in their lives.

It means a break from the stress and the routine and the monotony. Pretty much everyone is open to the opportunity to be entertained, regarding those individual differences which might hold them back from personal interactions.

Take the entertainer busking on the streets of a big city. Someone performing on the guitar and singing will attract attention from complete strangers, and these strangers will take a few minutes out of their busy lives to just stand and watch and appreciate the show.

Some buskers even make a decent amount of money when they are out, and people throw changes or bills into a hat or open guitar case.

People like entertainment, and, most of the time, the opportunity to be thrown out of their daily routines is a welcome reprieve from whatever stresses they are shouldering. Use this to your advantage.

Remember the guy who went around introducing himself to everyone in the room before approaching his target? He used this aspect of human nature to engage with people on their levels, whether they just wanted a good joke, someone to intently listen to their opinions or flattery.

You can pick up on what people want during the observational phase when you are analyzing how your targets react to different stimuli on a regular basis. It's a given that your access to your targets may be limited in different ways—but take advantage of the time you do have to observe them around other people.

The next common aspect of human behavior is the fact that, in modern-day society, people often adopt "masks" in public.

This mask refers to the persona that people set up in order to make good impressions on other people or to convey something about themselves based on what they want other people to think about them. Masks can be used for a variety of different purposes and to differing degrees.

Some people's public facades are vastly different from who they really are, while others' simply convey a mood and demeanor that conveys some singular aspect in line their intents.

Perhaps they wear a specific brand and dress a certain way in an effort to appear intelligent and noteworthy, while they would never dress that way in other circumstances.

Additionally, one of the most effective actions you can take is conveying to someone that you see who they "really" are. The initial reaction to this might be hesitation and noticeable vulnerability, but if you can make this transition while also ensuring that you can be trusted, and like what you see underneath the mask, then you will see an immediate change in the person's demeanor as they let down their guard and open themselves up to whatever it is you are offering.

At the very least, they will be inclined to listen, as they are intrigued. Getting your foot in the door is only the first step, however. So don't move straight into an aggressive interaction or go into sales mode.

Most people will be looking for a confirmation at this point that they have made an accurate reading of your character. Failing to provide this confirmation through your behaviors, words, and other actions will prompt that mask to go right back up, along with barriers. I'll demonstrate this through an example.

Your target is an attractive young lady in one of your college classes. She is an active member of lots of different school organizations and seems to be surrounded by people who are also well-established and who seem to be well connected.

She dresses smartly and conservatively, and she gains the status of "teacher's pet" in nearly every classroom she enters.

You are not so involved in the school, and you also don't consider yourself anywhere near as smart. However, you decide to put some effort into the investigation of this girl, let's call her Jessica.

She has a Facebook profile, and she is also listed under many rosters for student organizations in a variety of different academic fields.

She is majoring in business administration and takes elective courses in philosophy and European history. You assume from this information that these elective courses reflect a personal interest, as they are not directly aligned with her major. These are all valuable bits of information.

If you have not had a conversation with this girl in order to ascertain her other courses, you may have been able to find acquaintances of hers who give you this information as part of a casual, friendly conversation. Your first concern in any endeavor involving dark psychology techniques and manipulation is the art of casual conversation.

You should feel comfortable talking to people and be consistently aware of the appropriateness of the context in which you are approaching. Random, unplanned discussions on a college campus are certainly ordinary, and you may decide to put yourself on your target's radar by talking to her friends, or even starting a preparatory relationship through a simple conversation with a "stranger."

To set yourself up for this, simply pay attention to her movements throughout the campus and place yourself conveniently in the area when she is around. Perhaps you get in line at the same place in the cafeteria and start the conversation with a funny comment about the food. Keep this interaction short.

"How are you?"; "What's your major?"; and "What classes are you taking this semester?" are all innocent enough for this brief interaction, and if you end the conversation promptly after gathering a few tidbits of information, then you will probably not stay on Jessica's mind for long afterward, as she clearly around lots of people all the time, meeting and greeting.

However, if there was any kind of attraction coming from her side, then you may very well have made a better-than-expected impression, which is all the better for your purposes.

You want to simply plant an innocent seed which involved her knowing that you are around, and that, hopefully, you are entertaining to talk to casually. During this brief interaction, you want to pay attention to her behavior.

How receptive was she to speaking with you? What was her mood like? Was she hesitant? Open and friendly? Those who are more cautious about talking to people they don't know will require a more careful approach so as not to scare them off.

People who are generally open and friendly and love talking to new people will be much easier to approach in a successful way, assuming you don't do anything to cause them discomfort.

Once you've made all the observations you can about your target, Jessica, and have secured some type of scenario in which a conversation will feel natural and non-intimidating, then you are ready to make your crucial move in which you convey to her that you appreciate something about her which no one else really sees or understands.

You won't necessarily know the degree to which this will be true until your discussion, but you should try to steer the conversation based on the reactions you are getting from your target.

Remember the techniques we've discussed already, including cold reading and mirroring. Do what you can to reproduce her behavior so that she consciously and subconsciously registers you as someone who is "safe."

Also, use your information and analysis of her conduct and responses to speak as though you know more about her than you really do. Do not inundate her with this information, though; any sense of trust you've been able to conjure so far will be shattered if she were to start to suspect that you've been digging for information about her.

But if you can approach successfully according to her personality, then you will start to see some magic happening when you gradually introduce information that ties in with her more hidden interests.

Whatever you've been able to find out about which seems at odds with her external façade, introducing your commonalities in this regard will elicit one of several responses that you should use to guide your next comments.

If she hesitates and looks slightly uncomfortable, this is your warning sign of easing off a bit. She may be getting suspicious of how you happen to have information about her or how convenient it is that you have common interests.

Another way to try and safeguard yourself from a reaction like this is to adopt an interest that is not the same but similar or in the same realm as her interests.

Learn what you can about the interest and present this to her instead. This way, she will feel a comfortable distance and perhaps a higher degree of plausibility than if you said you were also interested in European history or some other hobby.

If Jessica's reaction is more one of intrigue and surprise, then you have prompted a more positive feeling towards your comments, and you can safely continue in this vein. Do not try to abruptly change the trajectory of the conversation and use this experience toward your mental notes as far as how to proceed.

There is another path along the route to uncovering a person's mask to get a positive reaction. If you are still in the process of discovering what is underneath a target's external but want to make an initial impression as far as perception, you can always employ the principle known as the "Barnum effect."

The Barnum effect is the phenomenon of people believing commonly applicable information as personal truths. Examples include things like that little horoscope paragraph telling you that you will "meet someone interesting in the next week" or that you will "have the opportunity to do something great within the next few days."

Statements like these have an alluring quality in that they seem too personalized advice, but in fact, they are widely applicable tidbits that can apply to a lot of different people all the time. The thing is, there is another rather universal tendency having to do with human nature and universal desire. We all like to feel special.

You can make your target feel unique by making "personal" suggestions or giving advice on a generalized scale that seems like you've put the time and effort into creating a specific, thought-provoking comment.

The fact that there are a lot of general comments you can make that will likely apply to the target perfectly means that you have some space to make an impression. Employing the Barnum effect in conjunction with a practiced strategy of cold reading can yield excellent results, as your skills have a chance to ignite a fascination with your seemingly exceptional skills at perception.

Being perceptive echoes back to the human desire to have people around who can pay attention and really listen to them when they are talking about things they care about.

When you can land this kind of impression without having the target tell you first makes an even more powerful interaction because it seems as though you've arrived at your impressions naturally and can relate on a personal level.

This is really at the foundation of much of humankind's deep well of desires, so play on this if it seems the cards have aligned for you.

Your next step is to pay attention to any changes in behavior over the course of multiple interactions. After you've made your initial connection, going back to the brief conversation in which you engaged for only a few minutes in a scenario where you "happen" to be in the same place at the same time, be sure to take mental notes—or physical notes—about how the interaction went.

When you make another effort at connection, pay attention to whether or not it seems she recognizes you from before. If she does, it will be either a positive recognition or a negative one, signaling that you've made a poor initial impression.

You will see her eyes light up if she received a positive impact from you before, and you will probably see more of a sneer and draining of energy for a moment if her perception of you was poor. This can change over time, so don't take a positive reaction entirely for granted.

You could still mess things up if you are too forward in a situation where she has yet reached that level of comfort with you. At the end of your second interaction, be sure to open the doorway for another contact in the future.

Depending on how well things are going, this could mean directly asking her out on a formal date. Or it could mean offering to spend some time with her studying or doing something else she enjoys doing.

If you can zero in on something that involves who she is under her mask, then this is ideal. Invite her to accompany you to a museum showcasing European history as a special exhibit, or invite her to go to a movie you think she'd like.

Something that sounds faintly flirtatious but not overtly like a come-on is a better way to go if you are unsure of where you stand at the end of this interaction.

Pay attention to her next words and the tone of voice she uses. She may try to backtrack awkwardly and throw out implausible excuses if she is uncomfortable with a date-type situation. So back off a bit and focus your effort towards re-establishing trust. If she accepts eagerly, then you've taken a big step forward in your pursuits.

Chapter 3: Microexpressions and Body Language

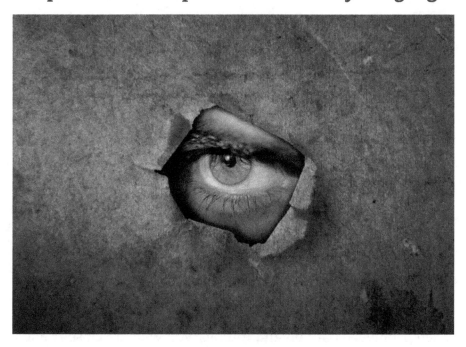

We've discussed many of the most important aspects of employing dark psychology methods and manipulation techniques. In this chapter, we will go even deeper into the art of gathering information and analyzing potential targets through careful attention to microexpressions and body language.

Listening to how a person talks and what he/she says in response to others is one facet of the art of manipulation, especially when employing dark psychology methods in conjunction with persuasion and other analysis techniques. However, it has been observed through research that what comes out of a person's mouth is only a fraction of what's going on in terms of human communication. Our subconscious minds are picking up on things that we do not notice consciously, and these may crop up on us later in ways we least expect them to.

But if we pay attention, we can learn to more consciously process how another person is conveying information through their microexpressions and body language. First, we will define these terms more thoroughly so that you understand what we're referring to. Then, we will look more in depth to how these signals manifest in different possible scenarios.

When people look at you and interact you who are close friends or people you've known for a long time, you may not realize that their definition of you and your behavior includes a whole lot of nonverbal communication that you may or may not be aware you're using.

You might be surprised, so some time ask your friends to describe what they see when they interact with you. They may make comments about your sense of humor and the kinds of comments you make, but you will also probably hear a lot about how you move when you talk, your facial expressions, and other mannerisms that are unique and specific to you.

These things are as closely associated with you like the words that you say. They are part of your personality, and they say a lot about you without your having to explain explicitly through verbal language.

This principle holds for pretty much all human beings. We've talked a lot about the need to observe and keep track of precise behaviors in order to gather information about a potential target.

But when it comes to up close and personal, there is a whole new world to pay attention to that will open a doorway to the person inside that your target is probably trying to hide to the best of their ability, assuming you are a brand new acquaintance.

Microexpressions are incredibly brief expressions which do not usually last long enough to register to the observer consciously. This is why they are called microexpressions. Sometimes, they're about hiding true feelings soon after letting an expression slip, and sometimes they are totally unconscious reactions to someone or something going in their environment.

They convey emotion just like regular facial expressions, but they are difficult to pick up unless you are really paying attention. Body language is everything going on with the body that is broadcasting information other than what is coming out of your mouth.

Those gestures you use when you talk, the furrowing of the eyebrows, and crossing of your legs or arms, all of these movements are communicating something or a variety of things to the careful observer, so it's essential to get a better understanding of what your body language is saying to other people around you, in addition to how to read the body language of others you are talking with.

This practice is especially important when you are meeting someone new. When you are looking to make a good first impression, noticing microexpressions and body language cues will help if you are working to employ the mirroring and cold readings techniques previously discussed.

Let's look at some of our previous examples and examine what's going on through the lens of microexpressions and paying attention to body language.

Remember Nichole from our example of the new guy at the party trying to make an impression? She is the alpha prize, and she is surrounded by people who are charmed by her personality and conversation. You have made significant moves in terms of winning over the room and have successfully attracted the attention of Nichole.

You have managed to secure a private conversation with her. We can imagine the two of you out on the balcony with a couple of drinks. What are your next moves?

The face is one of the most expressive parts of the human body and will tell you a lot if you pay attention. Obviously, common expressions like smiling or crying convey straightforward emotions in the general sense, but there are microexpressions going on, which come down the smallest movements of facial muscles.

Don't focus so hard on catching these that you end up staring and making your target feel uncomfortable; this would certainly be counterproductive. But definitely practice making effective eye contact so that you can take note of how Nichole is behaving and reacting, both when she is talking to you and when you are talking to her.

Again, too much eye contact equals staring and can come off as creepy, so practice other gestures and don't feel like looking around at your environment will convey disinterest, as long as there is a right balance.

What is going on between her smiles? Where are her eyes looking? When we are working hard to simulate an emotion or a mood, there will be little hints given off here and there in the form of microexpressions which can betray our real state of mind if someone notices them.

If you see any signs between her smiles that she is uncomfortable or disinterested, then you need to take note and change tactics, and quickly.

These signs may include things like looking down and letting off a smile briefly before conjuring it again, slouched posture, eyes that dart away from you, almost like she's looking for an exit, and pursed lips, similar to the way someone might look when they are tense or anxious.

Remember, she may be trying to be polite or to hide these feelings, so if you catch any signal that she is uncomfortable in some way, make a point to make some space between you two and change the subject as naturally as possible to something more general and less invasive. Perhaps you were asking personal questions you thought she would not mind answer, but then you received signals and hesitation before she spoke.

You might make a comment to reassure her that you don't want her to feel pressured and that you want her to be comfortable. Being straightforward and honest with your words, along with genuine concern, can do wonders when it comes to reversing uncomfortable or uneasy emotions.

Do what you can to turn things around so that she feels better, or, if nothing is really working at the moment, go ahead and end the interaction as natural as possible. You can always try again at another time.

There may something going on in her life that has nothing to do with you, but it is preventing her from fully engaging with you. Don't do anything that would endanger your chances of re-engaging with her in the future, if that is your intent. Sometimes, it's just a matter of timing, so you don't need to necessarily take it personally if you're not hitting things out of the ballpark in terms of chemistry and reciprocity.

Now, on the other hand, you may catch some positive signs that she is trying to hide how much she is enjoying the interaction. These are great if you see them, and they will reassure you that your tactics are working well to bring her to a place where she feels she can safely reveal personal information to you.

These signals manifest in different ways, but often include brief flashes of a wide grin that she quickly tries to tone down. She might be excited by the interaction and is trying to hide this, as she doesn't want to come off as easy.

She also might not want to make you uncomfortable, should she seem too eager during your interaction. On the other hand, keep in mind that a lot of people's response to anxiety is also excessive smiling and giggling, so look for signs that her smiles and hidden excitement impact the eyes when they happen.

Genuine smiles always affect the skin around the eyes. You can tell when someone is faking a smile because it does not reach the eyes.

You find this expression written often in novels when a writer is trying to convey that someone is not genuine and only pretending to be someone who is trustworthy or having fun.

Now, when it comes to body language, there are lots of things you can infer from everything from the way she's standing to where her feet are oriented.

Do your best to let her move naturally in order to gauge her mood and analyze how she feels about you. You might be surprised to know that you can almost tell everything you would need to know about a person and how she feels about you only by the way she is standing and holding herself while you are conversing with her.

The first thing you should look at is the way she is holding herself when you two have found a comfortable spot to have a conversation. If you are standing in a generally open space, what is her body's orientation in relation to yours?

The more her shoulders are oriented toward you, the more you can assess that she is interested in you and comfortable with sharing personal space. If her body is more like facing away from yours, then she is not entirely comfortable yet, and you should focus on steering the conversation towards the more comfortable and generalized ground until you can win some points back.

Body posture is any signifier that tells you if she is enjoying herself and is concerned about how she appears to you. If she is holding herself up straight and her head is facing you straight on when she is talking to you, then she is interested in keeping the conversation going.

When a person crosses their arms and/or their legs, it is often a subconscious signal that they are feeling uncomfortable or anxious and are moving to defend themselves or cover themselves up. This happens when someone feels like they've been exposed in some way, or when someone is trying to hide vulnerability and appear natural.

Look for these signs and pair them up in your mind with the words being spoken, and you should be able to guess pretty accurately what exactly she is feeling.

Feet orientation is something else to watch for, if you two are standing and not sitting with a table between you, that it. Feet that are oriented toward you would signify again that she is interested and feels comfortable exchanging information with you. If her feet or shoulders are oriented away from you, then she is not feeling so relaxed.

The further away is her angle of orientation from you, the more uncomfortable she feels with her surroundings. This should be taken as a strong signal that she is uninterested, and perhaps you should try again later.

Again, remember that there is always the possibility that something else is going on in her life that is affecting her sense of ease around people, so don't necessarily take it personally if she is conveying negative signals in response to your efforts.

Breathing and the rate at which someone is taking breaths will tell you about their level of comfort as well. Quick breaths usually signal that the person is uncomfortable and highly anxious, while natural, slow breathing signifies comfort.

If your target is expressing signs of discomfort, keep this in mind and tread carefully, and if nothing improves, then back off completely. But try not to make the disengagement awkward, as this will probably convey to her that you are uninterested and are put off by something she said or did.

If nothing else, you could also be honest and tell her that you are picking up on signs that she is uncomfortable. She may be intrigued and interested in hearing more, lowering her discomfort level! Nice job if you can pull that one-off.

Chapter 4: Personality Types

In our final chapter, we will give you the rundown of the 16 personality types as compiled by the famous Myers-Briggs personality tests and give you a starting point for studying and mastering how each of these types manifests itself in society.

The personality types are broken down into components. They are Sensing (S) – Intuition (N); Thinking (T) – Feeling (F); and Judging (J) – Perceiving (P). Before diving into the individual components and looking at the characteristics, let's first get a good idea of another couple of categories that will help you define another's personality type—introversion and extroversion.

You probably have a pretty good idea of what each of these terms means as they are both used widely and in many different contents. A person is generally considered an extrovert when his demeanor and personality tend to be outward facing.

He gets his energy from interaction with other people, and he enjoys being able to share experiences with other people. The extrovert tires quickly from being alone for too long of a period and will become lonely and in need of social interaction in order to feel stable, balanced, and happy again. On the other hand, there is the introvert.

An introvert gets her energy from spending time alone and taking a rest when lots of social interaction is demanded of her. She will tire quickly in energy-demanding social situations and feel the need to retire in order to "recharge" for the next social obligation on her schedule.

Most people have aspects of their personalities that fall into both categories, though they will mostly lean towards one or the other.

Sensing (S) – Intuition (I)

This scale is concerned with how and to what degree a person gathers information from the outside world. Sensing connotes just what it sounds like.

People who score higher in this category rely on their senses more than anything else in order to get information about their surroundings and make decisions.

They will also get strong emotional responses most often to stimuli that are gathered from the senses. More intuitive people like to think about abstract thoughts and spend a lot of time thinking about the future or creating ideas and thought patterns that are more philosophical and dependent upon impression.

They like to think about the possibilities rather than what they directly sense and will sometimes seem a bit fanciful in their interactions with others.

They are the kind of people you will see deeply engaged in a philosophical conversation at a party while everyone else is playing beer pong or trying to win at a board game.

Thinking (T) – Feeling (F)

This scale involves taking a look at how people make decisions once they've gathered date according to whichever side of the Sensing/Intuition scale they fall under.

Someone who is a deep thinker and dependent upon his thoughts in making a decision will tend to follow the facts and objective data as the primary source for his decision-making. He is factual, empirical data-driven person. Perhaps he is the practical nerd in class who is always cautioning people against specific actions based on the probability that the attempt will fail.

On the other hand, people who do a lot of feeling as they make decisions are probably more empathetic towards other people involved and what they are feeling to guide them. They will make "gut" decisions based on what they are feeling inside and according to their personal comfort levels.

They are usually more in touch with their inner feelings and convictions, and they might spend an excessive amount of time worrying about others and their problems, even before their own.

Judging (J) – Perceiving (P)

Those individuals who score higher on the judging side of this scale tend to favor quick, precise decisions based on snap judgments and strict convictions.

They may have a strong foundation of morals and established values against which they weigh nearly every decision and action that they are faced with. On the other hand, someone who is generally more perceptive in their dealings with the world will be open to new and variable possibilities to follow.

They are more willing to listen to another's input before making a firm decision on something or feeling a certain way.

They are generally more flexible in their daily practices, while the more judgmental individual might have a routine that is quite stressful for him when things get moved around.

The 16 Personality Types

The Inspector

The Inspector personality type is comprised of ISTJ personality sub-components. When you meet someone who is an inspector, the first thing you might notice is that this person seems to have everything together, to the last detail.

They are well organized and seem concerned with presenting themselves in a meticulous way to reflect their values, which often have a lot to do with being honorable and upholding justice, whatever his personal idea of justice happens to be.

These individuals will pose a challenge to the practitioner of dark psychology strategies, as you will have to get by a strong sense of moral character and judgment.

He will probably be able to pick up on your intentions should you trip up in even the slightest way. Be careful if your target is likely to fall into this category.

The Counselor

The counselor is a relatively rare personality type, and it is comprised of the components INFJ. You might recognize this personality type from unusual behaviors that may be eccentric, which reflects a quite profound and unique way of seeing the world.

They are usually very creative and imaginative, and your best bet for approaching the counselor type is to mirror their aspects of eccentricity. They will appreciate someone who might be a bit quirky but who seems to share her fascination with life imaginative way of thinking. The kindred soul might be the right approach here.

Another method, aside from sharing in a unique sense of the world, is expressing a shared interest of some kind. The counselor is likely to be very passionate about her hobbies or about her beliefs that she feels strongly.

Sharing her enthusiasm and passion is a great way to start some type of collaboration, which could be a good way in for your ultimate motives and goals for the relationship.

The Mastermind

The mastermind is comprised of the components INTJ, and they can be tricky to crack should you come across one whom you wish to create a friendship or relationship with to some end. This is because they are often characterized by being loners and prefer to be alone, especially when it comes to personal projects and career goals.

They are natural introverts and will drain quickly should you try to engage in an overly extroverted way. Do not scare this type away by being too much for him to handle.

Instead, approaching with caution and with guiding questions toward this person's work goals might be a successful way to get a conversation going that interesting enough to not be draining for the target.

Be sure to know your stuff, though—trying to invent a deep conversation off the cuff will quickly be identified, and this type will likely dismiss you and not reconsider.

The Giver

The Giver type is comprised of the personality components ENFJ. You will find that approaching and starting a conversation with someone who identifies as the Giver will be much easier than with many other types. This is because the Giver is usually very open and friendly.

She loves to interact and make new friends, and she may also love to share her ideas about the world and what it could be. They will reflect a lot of their beliefs in their personality and speeches, so carefully listen so that you can quickly mirror both their demeanor and passion for a better world.

Pay attention to their chosen vocations and listen to how they want to make the world a better place. Listen to what it is they care about and try to elaborate on this to create an even bigger, more impressive idea.

You will soon find this person attaching to the conversation as she follows the thread of imagination. She usually follows her gut feelings when it comes to people, so make sure you are on top of your game before making your approach so as to avoid turning her off to you by giving off a dishonest vibe.

The Craftsman

The Craftsman is another one likely to challenge someone with dark psychological ambitions. That is because the Craftsman is characterized by spontaneity, which he often hides from the world behind a well-crafted mask.

This type is comprised of components ISTP. The easiest way to get in good with someone who is a Craftsman is to familiarize yourself with their chosen vocations and keep your conversation centered around current events and developments in this arena.

The Craftsman is usually dedicated to some type of hobby or career but is also enthusiastic about trying new ideas and improving upon them. Meeting a likeminded Craftsman could be the surest way to engage and relate to someone of this personality combination.

The Provider

The Provider is someone who is likely to be the manipulator's bread and butter when it comes to techniques outlined in this book. Much of what you've learned has to do with creating an environment in which a person is likely to open up and relinquish valuable things like trust and personal information.

The Provider, comprised of the components ESFJ, is extraordinarily extroverted and a natural social butterfly. She also loves attention and is likely to respond very receptively to techniques and dark psychology strategies which utilize flattery and flirtation.

You'll have some fun if you choose to approach someone of this type. If you play your cards right, you will also be able to form a friendship quickly, from which there are many paths to take and many possibilities dependent upon your ultimate goals.

The Idealist

The Idealist personality type is comprised of components INFP. This type is another tricky one because of the nature of and degree of introverted demeanors. They prefer to be alone in general and spend a lot of time in their heads.

An approach to the idealist might be not to approach at all, but to attract them out of their safe hiding place by transforming yourself into someone he or she would be excited to talk to.

One strategy would be camouflage yourself thoroughly in the guise of someone with the same interests and thought patterns and then place yourself in their vicinity.

Maybe join a club he is in or a class that not a lot of people take. Put yourself within view, but do not approach, at least at first.

Give him time to come around. If he does, that means that your guise is attractive and stimulating enough for him to have dropped his introverted nature momentarily to approach you.

The Performer

The performer is labeled as such because these personality types also love to be in the spotlight. They are very skilled when it comes to people, and you may find that, though they are friendly and outgoing, they are also quite savvy when it comes to picking up on signals that someone is not who they are pretending to be.

This is another type you will want to really prepare yourself for so that you do not end up on their list of people not to interact with.

If her impression of you is negative, then this is likely to splash to lots of people who surround her as friends and colleagues, so if you fail miserably in this endeavor, it is best to remove yourself entirely from that social circle and find a new potential target. Her components are ESFP.

The Champion

The Champion is one type you don't want to try using any stereotypical approaches on. They are not generally interested in people who can be "read like a book" and enjoy working and living outside the norm, making their own way and their own rules.

They are perceptive people, so they will also be another type to quickly pick up on any weaknesses you might have in terms of betraying your true nature and intentions. Their components are ENFP.

The Doer

Approaching someone of the Doer personality type might require a little more leg work—literally. The like to take action and are often on their feet looking for bigger and brighter attractions to analyze.

They like to be in their heads, but they will also be attracted to the chance of sharing their ideas and exciting thoughts with other like-minded people. Share an adventure or invite her out to something interesting where she can get a good dose of deep conversation while also exploring something new. Her components are ESTP.

The Supervisor

The Supervisor personality type is comprised of components ESTJ. They are the people who adhere to and believe in rules and upholding what they believe is right.

They enjoy and get satisfaction out of helping and guiding others, and this may be the best way to create some type of relationship with the Supervisor.

Approaching him in a way that frames the interaction as if you are in need of help will engage their sense of helping out his fellow man. Convince him that he is needed and that you are asking humbly for his services in some way.

You can make this strategy more productive and meaningful for the Supervisor if you can manage to make him feel not only as though he is truly needed, but that you are someone of a good character who is worth helping out.

The Commander

The Commander is another personality type to whom an approach reflecting a follower is recommended. This is because this type likes to be in charge, and their components include ENTJ.

They are the type which best reflects society's tenets of good leadership, and they enjoy putting together solutions to solve a challenge while also being in charge of other people to get the job done.

Putting on the persona of a willing follower or worker is an ideal approach strategy here.

The Thinker

The Thinker may just be the most challenging of the personality types when it comes to utilizing dark psychology and manipulative techniques.

This is because the Thinker is smart. Really smart. And they're going to be able to tell when they are being lied to more times than not. An approach here would probably be most successful if it stems from a more genuine place.

Don't focus on feeding the Thinker lies or false information in order to sway their impressions or feelings. Instead, frame some aspect of yourself with the intent of conjuring attraction, intrigue, or interest from the Thinker.

See if you can get her to be the one to approach and start a conversation. From there, focus on conveying honest, genuine interest and knowledge in your chosen field. Preparation is key here. Her components are INTP.

The Nurturer

The Nurturer is comprised of components ISFJ. They victim approach to someone who is a nurturer will likely be the most effective, and you will find it easy to interact if you can manage to pull it off. The Nurturer is a natural philanthropist with a desire to help others.

She is generally enthusiastic about whatever she preoccupies herself with in regards to making the world a better place and will be receptive if you convey that you are in genuine need of counsel or a shoulder to cry on.

The Visionary

The Visionary is comprised of components ENTP. The visionary requires excitement and like-minded conversation. They are not going to suffer you with your small talk or flattery.

The key to a Visionary's heart is to, again, reflect their interests and offer them something unique that has to do their area of study or vocation. You've got to maintain a high level of energy here so that your target does not become bored.

And he will be the quickest to dismiss you should he detect any level of dishonesty or ulterior motive in your interactions with him.

The Composer

Our final type is the Composer, and their components are ISFP. The Composer may be challenging to break the ice with at first, but if you can engage them in a thoughtful conversation, then you will find them quickly opening up, presenting a whole different personality that looks a lot more like an extrovert than their defined introvert nature.

They will require stimulating conversation and an agenda that involves taking action and discovering something new.

Chapter 5: Influence Human Behavior

Influence refers to the ability to have an effect on the development, character, or the behavior of something or someone.

When defining influence, it is better to look at an example. Imagine times when campaigns are just around the corner, and many politicians (regarded as people with social status) take this chance to exert an influence over the voters so that they vote for them.

Here, fame and authority have amplified the influential capacity of the individual.

Another example might happen in the workplace, whereby you have employed an engineer that has more qualifications than the rest. This engineer might have a lot of influence over the rest of the engineers in the department.

Human Behavior

When you use the term "human behavior," you are talking about the expressed capacity for mental, physical, and social activity that is present during the various stages of human life.

Humans go through many growth phases, and each phase is characterized by various behavioral features. These phases run from prenatal to old age.

To make this clear to you, it is best to look at the various examples of human behavior. The first one is the typical one – language – which you grew up learning all your life, and then it became part of your routine.

Another example is the reaction to a comment that is left by someone when you decide to take a particular side, whether unintentionally or intentionally express human behavior.

Influence, Persuasion, Manipulation, and Coercion

If you want to be a person of influence, you need to be able to understand the various components. Let us look at the different elements of behavior and how it works.

Influence

This is the aspect of having a vision for a situation and then without the use of force, motivating someone to do as you wish.

Persuasion

This is the capability of presenting something in such a way that you make people to believe in information, or to motivate them to make a decision.

As you can see, both persuasion and influence involve a change in behavior and attitudes; the difference is how this change happens. When you try to change the other person's behavior using your actions and words, you are trying to persuade the person.

If you can change the characters and thoughts of the other person using your personality, then you are trying to influence them.

Influence is all about knowing the best outcome of a situation and then pushing someone to change that vision into a reality.

If you have been in an organization, then you must have worked with some leaders who can bring about the change they desire merely by using the power of their personalities without the need to use a lot of words to pass a concept across.

Such leaders have taken the time to build a lot of credibility and trust. On the other hand, persuasion refers to a way that you can sway another person's opinion and make them believe in some information – whether right or wrong.

Both these concepts share a similar objective – to change someone else's attitude or behavior.

Influence works via example, while persuasion requires that you communicate clearly what you want. When you change someone opinion by delivering your case in a convincing way, you are persuading them. When you make people change their feelings, behavior, and attitudes due to your personality, you are influencing them.

This book works from the definition of persuasion being the act of convincing other people to take action without having gained their trust.

On the other hand, we look at influence as the ability to change the behavior of someone using actions that you have used to demonstrate over time.

We can look at manipulation as the distant cousin of persuasion and influence. Manipulation has to do with intention and purpose. Manipulation is defined as the controlling of human behavior using unfair or artful means to your advantage.

Manipulation is the attempt by a person to make the other person conduct himself in a specific manner to achieve his own goals. In most cases, manipulation makes use of unethical means to achieve the ends.

Manipulation often occurs when the manipulator takes over the right to take over the entire aspect of the life of another person, which can include the privacy of the person.

In a nutshell, manipulation is all about having your way. If you have kids, then you have experienced manipulation at its best because they are good at it.

Manipulation is also about placing a skin around the thing that you do so that you make it more effective and reduce the detection rate. The person you are trying to manipulate doesn't need to know what you are doing; otherwise, you won't succeed at the effort.

Manipulation can also be turned into reverse psychology. For instance, you use this on your kids when you tell them to eat up all their greens; otherwise, they will not become big and strong like their brothers.

This practice doesn't only work with kids; even older people can be easily convinced to do things that they didn't plan. When they don't want to do something, then you go ahead to huff and puff till they do it.

Influence and manipulation form the two sides of the same coin. On one side, manipulation is out to help others improve their behavior, while on the other side; manipulation is all about unfairness and deception.

The difference between the two boils down to your motivation as the change agent. On one part, manipulation is usually defined by the subject. If the other person feels that they are being manipulated, then you are definitely doing it.

However, influence can turn into manipulation very fast. For instance, if you find out that the only way to make someone change is to trick them into doing it, then you are manipulating them.

When you deceive the subject into taking that action that isn't in their best interest at all, then you have crossed the line from influence into manipulation.

Another instance when you cross the line into manipulation is when you plan to implement a change, regardless of what the outcome is.

You usually move ahead with the cause regardless of what other people think. This is akin to bulldozing them.

Finally, if you are serving your own interests in the hope that it goes your own way, and then you have jumped from being influential into being manipulative.

Coercion

Coercion is the last element we look under the influence of behavior, and is also termed as a mind-control technique. It comes in two forms – active and passive.

Passive coercion doesn't require you to do anything - all you need to do is to set up the right environment for something to happen. Your subject passes through this environment, and this simple act will end up influencing his behavior.

This is commonly seen when you walk into a large shopping mall. Everything has been set up to influence your decisions.

The main reason why passive coercion is such a success is that it is invisible. You aren't aware that the environment has been designed to make you perform specific tasks and actions or think certain thoughts.

For instance, when you enter a casino, you will notice cameras everywhere, and your thought is that they only there to make sure you are secure, but behind the cameras is a team of psychologists to study your behavior and take steps to keep you within the casino for longer so that you can spend more.

Active coercion, on the other hand, requires that you do everything in your power to make things work for you.

Human behavior is a complex subject that is deep as it is wide. Understanding human behavior needs you to learn various skills, and then when you decide to influence the behavior, you ought to look at the multiple aspects that make it possible for you to have an impact on someone.

Human behavior refers to the character of a person. You adopt the behavior as you grow – from your parents, school, peers, and other people in the community.

This is why you have heard so often it is mentioned that someone is of "good" or "bad" behavior. The way you behave right away tells someone a little about your upbringing.

The good thing is that you can change your behavior; however, it takes more than just stopping something for a few hours or days – it takes all your willpower and effort to change your behavior.

Let us look at the factors that can make someone change their behavior:

Willpower

Before someone can decide to change their behavior, they should genuinely want to change it. They need to have the willpower to make decisions and stick to them. When someone has the desire to change, they discipline themselves to follow the plans through.

Changing behavior starts with a plan, and when you have the desire to change the behavior, you need the strength to stick to this plan even when you feel like giving up.

It also works the other way round, in order for you to persuade someone to change their behavior; they need to be willing to do so; otherwise, you will be wasting your time.

Knowledge and Skills

When you come up with plans to do something, you need to have the knowledge and skills to succeed. For instance, when you decide to lose weight, yet you don't have the expertise to do so, you might end up failing.

With the right skills and knowledge to achieve a decision, you will be able to direct your willpower more effectively.

To apply this aspect, you need to try and educate the people that you are trying to persuade so that they have the right knowledge to handle the issue at hand.

They need to commit to a plan that will give them the right results. After they put the plan in motion, the next step is to make sure they can monitor their progress the right way.

Social Motivation

This is another prime factor that influences the way we act. Most of us have evolved to fit in a crowd because this crowd has helped us to stay safe.

Many people around you will help you to stay motivated and accountable, while others will seek to make you stray from your goals.

When persuading people, you need to help them realize that the people around them can be their allies or accomplices when they pursue their goals. Make sure you teach them how to communicate with the people around them well.

Social Ability

This is the capacity to accomplish something that you have never done through finding someone that has already done it before successfully. This means looking for a mentor, a support group, or a coach to guide you.

This is why, as a persuasion expert, you are there to help someone find his footing so as to change behavior.

Conclusion

There are many different personality types in the world, and you now have a better understanding of what those various personality components, how they work together, and how you can identify them through straightforward interactions and analysis.

You understand how cold reading works, and you are anything but gullible when it comes to people trying to convince you that they know more about you than you think.

You will be able to pick up on this immediately and have learned how people plant the seeds in others' minds to convince them that they have knowledge above and beyond what they actually possess.

A lot more is going on when two people meet for the first time than most people pick up on. Many people are so preoccupied with themselves and other thoughts that they would never notice the subtle cues that people are continually giving off, broadcasting their feelings and thoughts.

When you know the tricks of the trade when it comes to picking up nonverbal communication and body language, you will be able to read a great deal about people before they even open their mouths to introduce themselves. When you can read the room and size people up, you already have an advantage over anyone else who might be trying to vie for that person's affection, political support, or sales transaction.

It's impossible to become comfortable with these techniques without observation and practice. You will find that the more confident you are with your strategies, the more comfortable and more natural they will happen, leaving your targets entirely in the dark about what's going on under the surface.

Finally, you were introduced to the 16 different personality types, which are part of the Myers-Briggs personality analysis.

Perhaps you were convinced to go ahead and take the test yourself to get a better idea of which personality traits you most exhibit.

Now that you know more, you can continue your research into how these traits interact and what your inherent strengths and vulnerabilities might be.

Many people remain blind to the weaknesses that they seek to ignore for as long as possible. Knowing yourself is the best way to begin constructing how you will operate in terms of getting what you want out of any situation.

If there is one thing you've taken away from this book more than anything else, it is my hope that you've become much more confident in your own ability to recognize and fend off those who might wish to harm you in some way through the practice of manipulative techniques and other tools of dark psychology.

As has been stated many times throughout this book, I hope you value the fact that you've become much more knowledgeable and capable of identifying when someone is trying to use you or hurt you for their own gain.

You should now feel that you can recognize the sociopath, narcissist, or even the psychopath in the room should there be one, and you consequently know to stay as far away as possible.

CPSIA information can be obtained
at www.ICGtesting.com
Printed in the USA
BVHW080804050521
606421BV00006B/1726